My First
HAITIAN CREOLE
DICTIONARY

ENGLISH-HAITIAN CREOLE

Designed and edited by Maria Watson
Translated by Nathan Vertilus

Hippocrene Books, Inc.
New York

My First Haitian Creole Dictionary

English-Haitian Creole

Hippocrene Books, Inc. edition, 2019

For information, address:
HIPPOCRENE BOOKS, INC.
171 Madison Avenue
New York, NY 10016
www.hippocrenebooks.com

ISBN: 978-0-7818-1400-3

© Publishers

First edition, 2019

Published by arrangement with Biblio Bee Publications, an imprint of ibs Books (UK)
56, Langland Crescent, Stanmore HA7 1NG, U.K.

Printed at Star Print-O-Bind, New Delhi-110 020 (India)

Aa

actor

aktè *akteh*

actress

aktris *aktrees*

adult

granmoun
granhmoon

aeroplane
US English **airplane**

avyon *avyonh*

air conditioner

klimatizè
kleemateezeh

air hostess
US English **flight attendant**

otès delè
otehsdeleh

airport

ayewopò
ayewopoh

album

albòm *albohm*

almond

zanmann
zanhmanhn

alphabet

alfabè *alfabeh*

ambulance

anbilans
anhbeelanhs

angel

zanj *zanhj*

animal

zannimo
zanhneemo

ankle

cheviy *cheviy*

ant

foumi *foomee*

antelope

antilòp *antilohp*

antenna

antèn *anhtehn*

apartment

apatman
apatmanh

ape

makak *makak*

apple

pòm *pohm*

apricot

abriko *abreecko*

apron

tabliye *tableeye*

aquarium

akwaryòm
akwaryohm

a b c d e f g h i j k l m n o p q r s t u v w x y z

archery

tiralak *teeralak*

architect

achitèk *acheetehk*

arm

bra *bra*

armour
US English **armor**

zam *zam*

arrow

flèch *flehch*

artist

atis *atees*

asparagus

aspèj *aspehj*

astronaut

astwonòt *astwonòt*

astronomer

astwonòm *astwonohm*

athlete

atlèt *atleht*

atlas

atlas *atlas*

aunt

matant *matanht*

author

otè   *oteh*

automobile

oto   *oto*

autumn

lotòn   *lotohn*

avalanche

lavalas   *lavalas*

award

prim   *preem*

axe

rach   *rach*

Bb

baby

ti bebe   *teebebe*

back

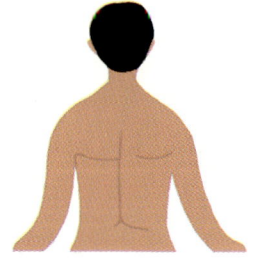

do   *do*

bacon

la kochon
lakochonh

badge

badj   *badj*

badminton

badminton
badmeenton

bag

valiz   *valeez*

baker

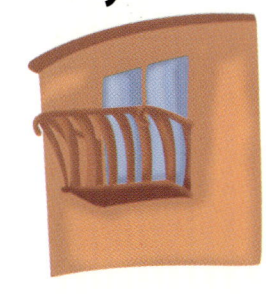

bòs pen   *bohspenh*

balcony

balkon   *balkonh*

bald

chòv   *chohv*

ball

boul   *bool*

ballerina

dansez balè
danhsezbaleh

balloon

balon   *balonh*

bamboo

banbou   *banhboo*

banana

bannann
banhnanhn

band

bann   *banhn*

bandage

bandaj   *banhdaj*

barbeque

babekyou
babekyoo

a **b** c d e f g h i J k l m n o p q r s t u v w x y z

a
b
c
d
e
f
g
h
i
j
k
l
m
n
o
p
q
r
s
t
u
v
w
x
y
z

barn

galata   *galata*

barrel
barik   *bareek*

baseball
bezbòl   *bezbohl*

basket
pànye   *panye*

basketball

baskètbòl
baskehtbohl

bat
chovsouri
chovsooree

bath
benwa   *benwa*

battery
batri   *batree*

bay
bè   *beh*

beach

plaj   *plaj*

beak

bèk   *behk*

bean

pwa   *pwa*

bear

lous *loos*

beard

bab *bab*

bed

kabann *kabanhn*

bee

myèl *myehl*

beetle

skarabe *skarabe*

beetroot

bètrav *behtrav*

bell

klòch *klohch*

belt

sentiwon *sinhteewonh*

berry

bè *beh*

bicycle

bisiklèt *beeseekleht*

billiards
US English **pool**

biya *beeya*

bin

poubèl *poobehl*

a
b
c
d
e
f
g
h
i
J
k
l
m
n
o
p
q
r
s
t
u
v
w
x
y
z

bird

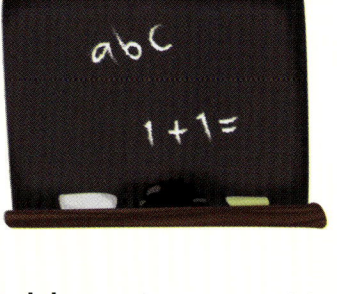

zwazo   *zwazo*

biscuit

biskwit   *beeskweet*

black

nwa   *nwa*

blackboard

tablo   *tablo*

blanket

dra   *dra*

blizzard

tanpèt nèj
tanhpehtnehj

blood

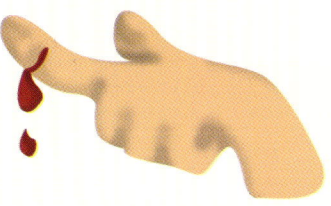

san   *sanh*

blue

ble   *ble*

boat

bato   *bato*

body

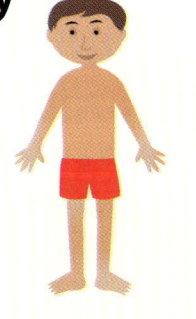

kò   *koh*

bone

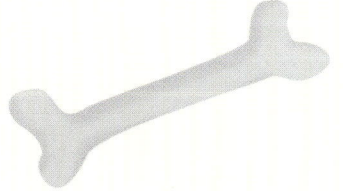

zo   *zo*

book

liv   *leev*

boot
bòt   *boht*

bottle
boutèy   *bootehy*

bow
wozèt   *wozeht*

bowl
bòl   *bohl*

box
bwat   *bwat*

boy
gason   *gasonh*

bracelet
braslè   *brasleh*

brain
sèvo   *sehvo*

branch
branch   *branhch*

bread
pen   *pinh*

breakfast
manje maten
manhjematinh

brick
brik   *breek*

a
b
c
d
e
f
g
h
i
J
k
l
m
n
o
p
q
r
s
t
u
v
w
x
y
z

bride

lamarye
lamarye

bridegroom

mesye marye
mesyemarye

bridge

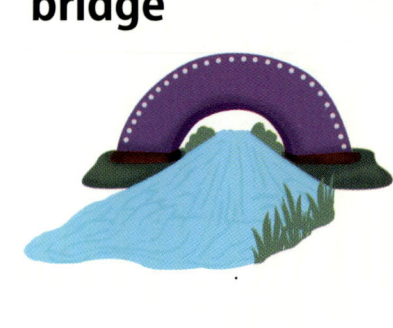

pon
ponh

broom

bale
bale

brother

frè
freh

brown

mawon
mawonh

brush

bwòs
bwohs

bubble

blad
blad

bucket

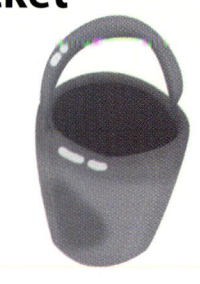

bokit
bokeet

buffalo

bifalo
beefalo

building

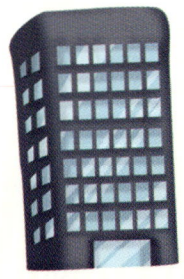

bilding
beelding

bulb

anpoul
anhpool

bull

towobèf   *towobehf*

bun

briyòch   *breeyohch*

bunch

pake   *pake*

bundle
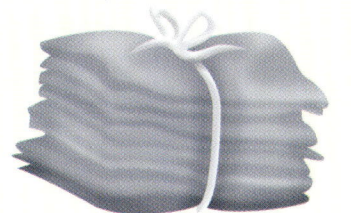
pakèt   *pakeht*

bungalow

bangalou
banhgaloo

burger

anmbègè
anmbehgeh

bus

bis   *bees*

bush

toufbwa   *toofbwa*

butcher

bouche   *booche*

butter

bè   *beh*

butterfly

papiyon
papeeyonh

button
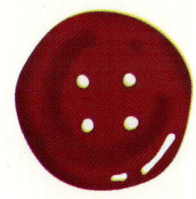
bouton   *bootonh*

Cc

cabbage

chou *choo*

cabinet

kabinè *kabeeneh*

cable

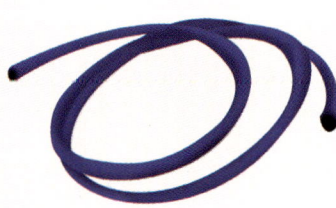

kab *kab*

cable car

machin a kab *macheen a kab*

cactus

kaktis *kaktees*

cafe

kafe *kafe*

cage

kaj *kaj*

cake

gato *gato*

calculator

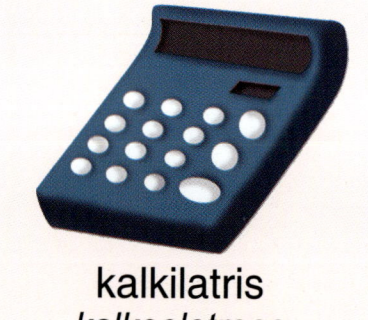

kalkilatris *kalkeelatrees*

calendar

kalandriye *kalanhdreeye*

calf

ti bèf *teebehf*

camel

chamo *chamo*

camera

kamera *kamera*

camp

kan *kanh*

can

bwat *bwat*

canal

kannal *kanhnal*

candle

chandèl
chanhdehl

canoe

kanoy *kanoy*

canteen

kantin *kanhteen*

cap

kepi *kepee*

captain

kapitèn
kapeetehn

car

machin *macheen*

caravan

karavàn *karavan*

card

kat *kat*

carnival

kanaval *kanaval*

carpenter

bòs chapant
bohs chapanht

carpet

tapi *tapee*

carrot

kawòt *kawoht*

cart

kabwa *kabwa*

cartoon

ti komik *teekomeek*

cascade

kaskad *kaskad*

castle

chato *chato*

cat

chat *chat*

caterpillar

cheni *chenee*

cauliflower

chouflè *choofleh*

a b c d e f g h i j k l m n o p q r s t u v w x y z

cave
gwòt *gwoht*

ceiling
plafon *plafonh*

centipede
santimyè *santeemyeh*

centre
US English **center**
mitan *meetanh*

cereal
sereyal *sereyal*

chain
chèn *chehn*

chair
chèz *chehz*

chalk
lakrè *lakreh*

cheek
bò machwè *bohmachweh*

cheese
fwomaj *fwomaj*

chef
chèf *chehf*

cherry
seriz *sereez*

a b c d e f g h i J k l m n o p q r s t u v w x y z

chess

echèk *echehk*

chest

pwatrin *pwatreen*

chick

ti poul *teepool*

chilli
US English **chili**

piman *peemanh*

chimney

chemine
chemeene

chin

manton *manhtonh*

chocolate

chokola *chokola*

Christmas

fèt nwèl *feht nwehl*

church

legliz *legleez*

cinema

sinema *seenema*

circle

sèk *sehk*

circus

sik *seek*

city

lavil *laveel*

classroom

sal klas *sal klas*

clinic

klinik *kleeneek*

clock

revèy *revehy*

cloth

twal *twal*

cloud

nwaj *nwaj*

clown

kloun *kloon*

coal

chabon *chabonh*

coast

kot *kot*

coat

manto *manhto*

cobra

kobra *kobra*

cockerel

US English **rooster**

ti kòk *teekohk*

a b **c** d e f g h i j k l m n o p q r s t u v w x y z

cockroach

ravèt *raveht*

coconut

kokoye *kokoye*

coffee

kafe *kafe*

coin

piès kòb
piehs kohb

colour
US English **color**
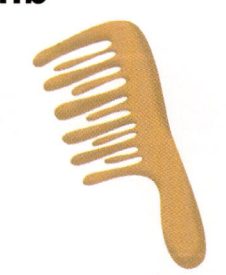

koulè *kooleh*

comb

peny *pinhy*

comet

komèt *komeht*

compass

konpa *konhpa*

computer

òdinatè
ohdeenateh

cone

kón *kon*

container

veso *veso*

cook

kizinyè
keezeenyeh

cookie
bonbon
bonhbonh

cord
kòd
kohd

corn
mayi
mayee

cot
bèso
behso

cottage
ti kay
teekay

cotton
koton
kotonh

country
peyi
peyee

couple
koup
koop

court
tribinal
treebeenal

cow
bèf
behf

crab
krab
krab

crane
machin pou leve bagay lou
macheen poo leve bagay loo

a b **c** d e f g h i J k l m n o p q r s t u v w x y z

crayon

kreyonkoulè
kreyonhkooleh

crocodile

kwokodil
kwokodeel

cross

kwa   *kwa*

crow

kònèy   *kohnehy*

crowd

foul moun
fool moon

crown

kouwòn   *koowohn*

cube

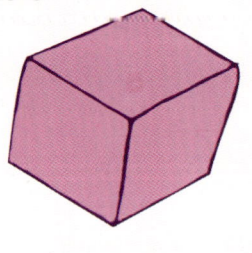

kib   *keeb*

cucumber

konkonm
konhkonhm

cup

tas   *tas*

cupboard

kòf   *kohf*

curtain

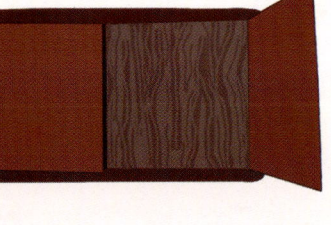

rido   *reedo*

cushion

kousen   *koosinh*

Dd

dam

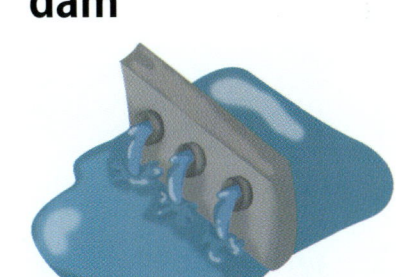

baraj *baraj*

dancer

dansè *danhseh*

dart

flèch *flehch*

data

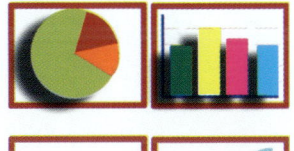

done *done*

dates

dat *dat*

daughter

pitit fi
peeteet fee

day

jou *joo*

deck

jwèt kat *jweht kat*

deer

sèf *sehf*

den

tou wòch
toowohch

dentist

dantis *danhtees*

a b c **d** e f g h i J k l m n o p q r s t u v w x y z

desert

dezè *dezè*

design

dizay *deezay*

desk
biwo *beewo*

dessert

desè *deseh*

detective
detektif *detekteef*

diamond

dyaman *dyamanh*

diary
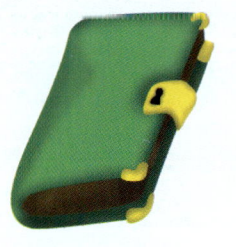
jounal *joonal*

dice
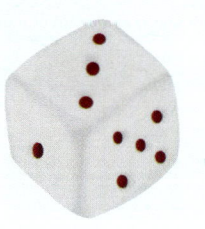
zo *zo*

dictionary

diksyonè *deeksyoneh*

dinosaur

dinozò *deenozoh*

disc
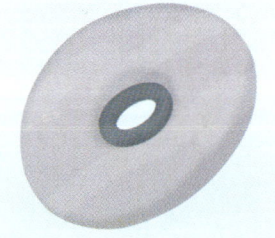
disk *deesk*

dish

plat *plat*

diver

plonjè   *plonhjeh*

dock

waf   *waf*

doctor

doktè   *dokteh*

dog

chen   *chinh*

doll

poupe   *poope*

dolphin

dofen   *dofinh*

dome

dom   *dom*

domino

domino   *domeeno*

donkey

bourik   *booreek*

donut

beyè   *beyeh*

door

pòt   *poht*

dough

pat farin
pat fareen

dragon

dragon *dragonh*

drain

dren *drinh*

drawer

tiwa *teewa*

drawing

fè desen *feh desinh*

dream

rèv *rehv*

dress

wòb *wohb*

drink

bwason *bwasonh*

driver

chofè *chofeh*

drop

gout *goot*

drought

sechrès *sechrehs*

drum

tanbou *tanhboo*

duck

kanna *kanhna*

dustbin
US English **trash can**

poubèl *poobehl*

duvet

kwèt *kweht*

dwarf

tinen *teeninh*

Ee

eagle

malfini *malfeenee*

ear

zòrèy *zohrehy*

earring

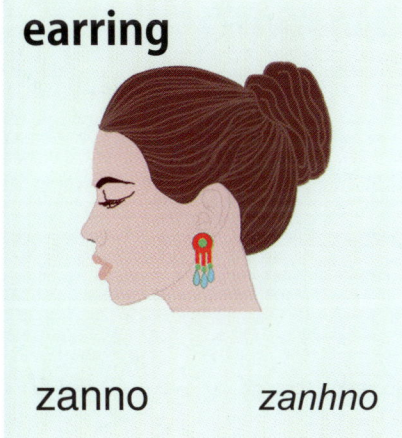

zanno *zanhno*

earth

latè *lateh*

earthquake

tranblemandtè *tranhblemanhdteh*

earthworm

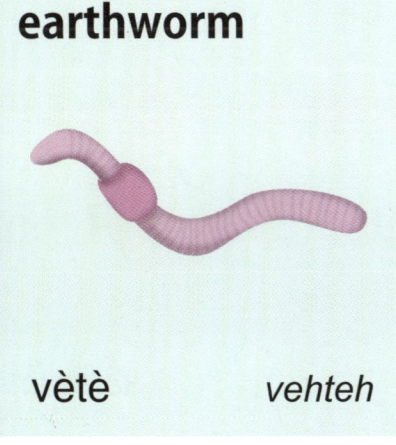

vètè *vehteh*

eclipse

eklips *ekleeps*

edge

lizyè *leezyeh*

27

eel

zangi · *zanhgee*

egg

ze · *ze*

eight

uit · *ueet*

elastic

elastik · *elasteek*

elbow

koud · *kood*

electrician

elektrisyen · *elektreesyinh*

electricity

elektrisite · *elektreeseete*

elephant

elefan · *elefanh*

elevator

asansè · *asanhseh*

elf

èlf · *ehlf*

email

imèl · *eemehl*

embroidery

bwodri · *bwodree*

engine
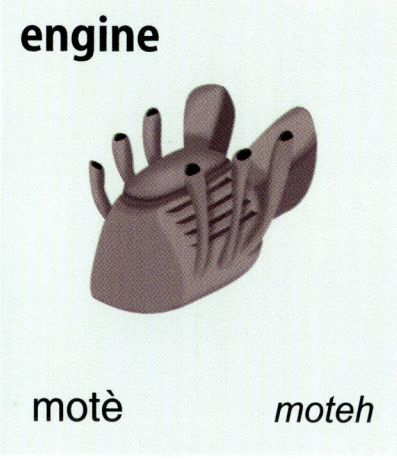
motè *moteh*

entrance
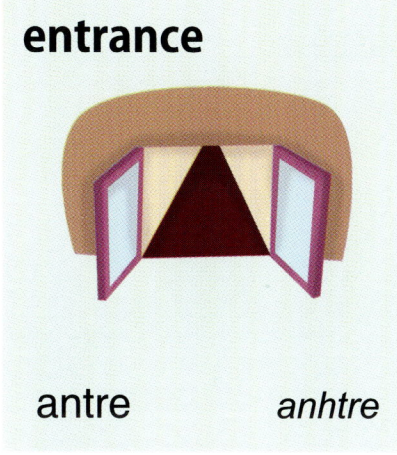
antre *anhtre*

envelope
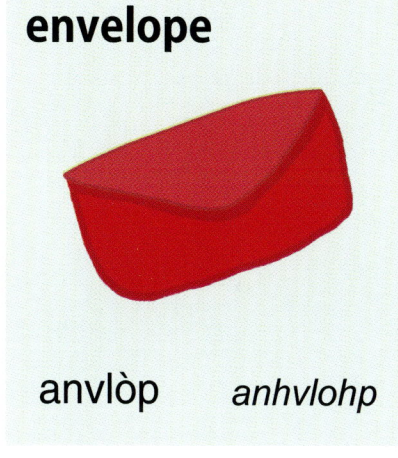
anvlòp *anhvlohp*

equator
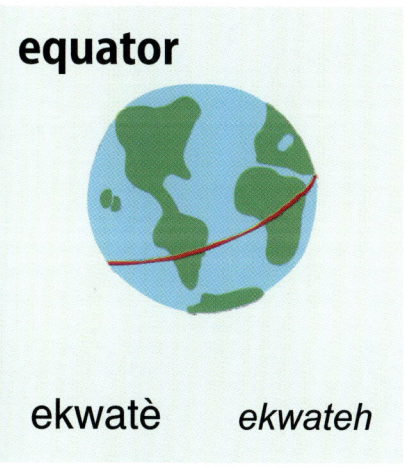
ekwatè *ekwateh*

equipment
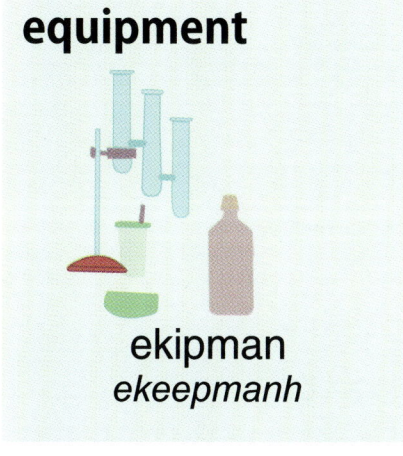
ekipman *ekeepmanh*

eraser
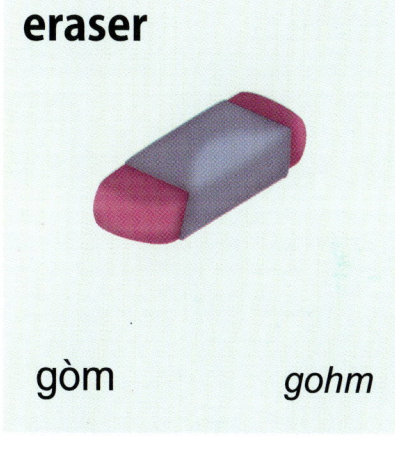
gòm *gohm*

escalator
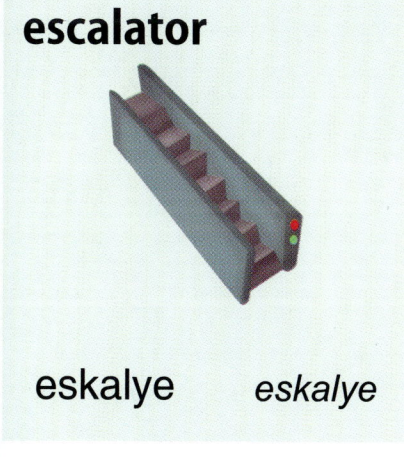
eskalye *eskalye*

eskimo

eskimo *eskeemo*

evening

aswè *asweh*

exhibition

egzibisyon *egzeebeesyonh*

eye
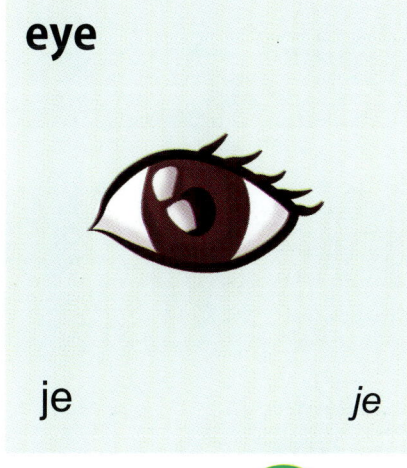
je *je*

eyebrow
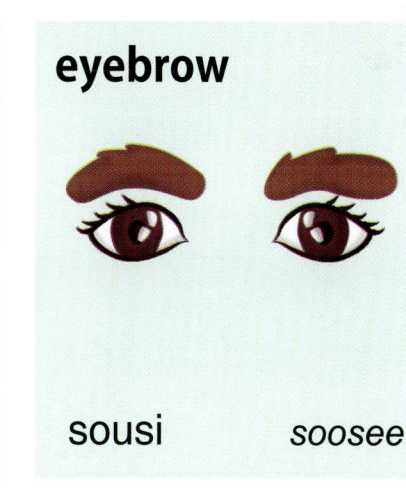
sousi *soosee*

a b c d **e** f g h i J k l m n o p q r s t u v w x y z

Ff

fabric

tisi *teesee*

face

figi *feegee*

factory

faktori *faktoree*

fairy

fe *fe*

family

fanmi *fanhmee*

fan

vantilatè *vanhteelateh*

farm

fèm *fehm*

farmer

kiltivatè *keelteevateh*

fat

gra *gra*

father

papa *papa*

feather

plim *pleem*

female

femèl   *femehl*

fence

kloti   *klotee*

ferry

feri   *feree*

field

jaden   *jadinh*

fig

fig   *feeg*

file

dosye   *dosye*

film

fim   *feem*

finger

dwèt   *dweht*

fire

dife   *deefe*

fire engine

kamyon ponpye
kamyonh ponhpye

firefighter

ponpye   *ponhpye*

fireworks

fedatifis
fedateefees

a b c d e **f** g h i J k l m n o p q r s t u v w x y z

fish

pwason   *pwasonh*

fist

pwen   *pwinh*

five

senk   *sinhk*

flag

drapo   *drapo*

flame

flanm dife
flanhm deefe

flamingo

flaman woz
flamanh woz

flask

flakon   *flakonh*

flock

twoupo   *twoopo*

flood

inondasyon
eenonhdasyonh

floor

etaj   *etaj*

florist

fleris   *flerees*

flour

farin   *fareen*

flower

flè *fleh*

flute

flit *fleet*

fly

mouch *mooch*

foam

kim *keem*

fog

bwouya *bwooya*

foil

fèy metalik
fehy metaleek

food

manje *manhje*

foot

pye *pye*

football
US English **soccer**

foutbòl *footbohl*

forearm

avanbra *avanhbra*

forehead

fwon *fwonh*

forest

forè *foreh*

a b c d e f g h i j k l m n o p q r s t u v w x y z

fork

fouchèt   *foocheht*

fortress

fòtrès   *fohtrehs*

fountain

sous dlo   *soos dlo*

four

kat   *kat*

fox

rena   *rena*

frame

ankadreman
anhkadremanh

freezer

frizè   *freezeh*

fridge
US English **refrigerator**

frijidè   *freejeedeh*

friend

zanmi   *zanhmee*

frog

krapo   *krapo*

fruit

fwi   *fwee*

fumes

lafimen   *lafeemenh*

funnel

antonwa
anhtonwa

furnace

founo dife
foono deefe

furniture

mèb   *mehb*

Gg

gadget

gadjèt   *gadjeht*

gallery

galeri   *galeree*

game

jwèt   *jweht*

gap

fant   *fanht*

garage

garaj   *garaj*

garbage

fatra   *fatra*

garden

jaden   *jadenh*

garland

giland   *gueelanhd*

a
b
c
d
e
f
g
h
i
J
k
l
m
n
o
p
q
r
s
t
u
v
w
x
y
z

garlic

lay *lay*

gas

gaz *gaz*

gate

baryè *baryeh*

gem

pyè presye *pyeh presye*

generator

jeneratris *jeneratrees*

germ

jèm *jehm*

geyser

jeyzè *jeyzeh*

ghost

zonbi *zonhbee*

giant

jeyan *jeyanh*

gift

kado *kado*

ginger

jenjanm *jenhjanhm*

giraffe

jiraf *jeeraf*

girl

tifi   *teefee*

glacier

glasye   *glasye*

glass

vè   *veh*

glider

planè   *planeh*

globe

glòb   *glohb*

glove

gan   *ganh*

glue

lakòl   *lakohl*

goal

gòl   *gohl*

goat

kabrit   *kabreet*

gold

lò   *loh*

golf

gòlf   *gohlf*

goose

zwa   *zwa*

a b c d e f **g** h i J k l m n o p q r s t u v w x y z

gorilla

goril *goreel*

grain

grenn *grenhn*

grandfather

granpapa
granhpapa

grandmother

grann *granhn*

grape

rezen *rezenh*

grapefruit

chadèk *chadehk*

grass

zèb *zehb*

grasshopper

sotrèl *sotrehl*

gravel

gravye *gravye*

green

vèt *veht*

grey

gri *gree*

grill

griy *greey*

grocery

makèt — *makeht*

ground

tè — *teh*

guard

sekirite — *sekeereete*

guava

gwayav — *gwayav*

guide

gid — *gueed*

guitar

gita — *geeta*

gulf

gòlf — *gohlf*

gun

zam — *zam*

gypsy

jitan — *jeetanh*

Hh

hair

cheve — *cheve*

hairbrush

bwòs tèt — *bwòs teht*

a b c d e f g h i j k l m n o p q r s t u v w x y z

hairdresser

kwafè　　*kwafeh*

half

mwatye　　*mwatye*

hall

koridò　　*koreedoh*

ham

janbon　　*janhbonh*

hammer

mato　　*mato*

hammock

amak　　*amak*

hand

men　　*menh*

handbag

ti valiz　　*tee valeez*

handicraft

atizana　　*ateezana*

handkerchief

mouchwa
moochwa

handle

manèt　　*maneht*

hanger

sèso　　*sehso*

40

harbour
US English **harbor**

pò   *poh*

hare

lapen   *lapenh*

harvest

rekòt   *rekoht*

hat

chapo   *chapo*

hawk

malfini   *malfeenee*

hay

pay   *pay*

head

tèt   *teht*

headphone

kas   *kas*

heap

pil   *peel*

heart

kè   *keh*

heater

aparèy chofaj
aparehy chofaj

hedge

kloti natirèl
klotee nateerehl

heel

talon *talonh*

helicopter

elikoptè *eleekopteh*

helmet

kask *kask*

hen

manman *manhmanh*

herb

zèb *zehb*

herd

kolonn *kolonhn*

hermit

èmit *ehmeet*

hill

ti mòn *tee mohn*

hippopotamus

ipopotam *eepopotam*

hive

nich myèl *neech myehl*

hole

twou *twoo*

honey

siromyèl *seeromyehl*

hood

kapo *kapo*

hook

kwòk *kwohk*

horn

kòn *kohn*

horse

chwal *chwal*

hose

konbèlann *konhbehlanhn*

hospital

lopital *lopeetal*

hotdog

sosis *sosees*

hotel

otèl *otehl*

hour

èdtan *ehdtan*

house

kay *kay*

human

moun *moon*

hunter

chasè *chaseh*

a b c d e f g **h** i j k l m n o p q r s t u v w x y z

43

hurricane

siklòn *seeklohn*

husband

mari *maree*

hut

joupa *joopa*

Ii

ice

glas *glas*

iceberg

aysbèg *ayzbehg*

ice cream

krèm glase
krehm glase

idol

zidòl *zeedohl*

igloo

iglou *eegloo*

inch

pous *poos*

injection

piki *peekee*

injury

blese *blese*

ink

lank *lanhk*

inn

obèj *obehj*

insect

ensèk *enhsehk*

inspector

enspektè *enhspekteh*

instrument

enstriman *enhstreemanh*

internet

entènèt *enhtehneht*

intestine

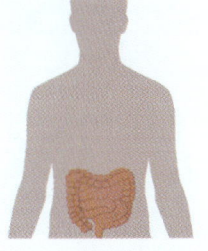

entesten *enhtestenh*

inventor

envantè *enhvanhteh*

invitation

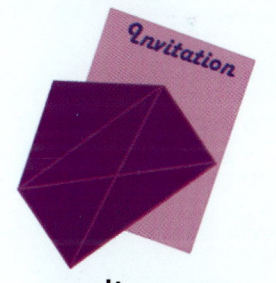

envitasyon *enhveetasyonh*

iron

fè a repase *feh a repase*

island

zile *zeele*

ivory

kòn elefan *kohn elefanh*

Jj

jackal

chakal   *chakal*

jacket

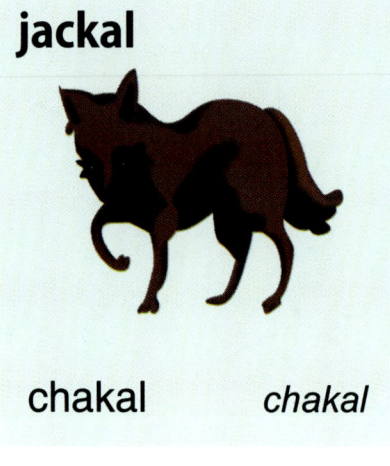

jakèt   *jakeht*

jackfruit

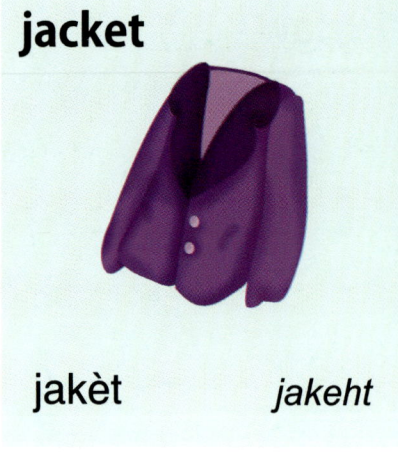

djaka   *djaka*

jam

konfiti   *konhfeetee*

jar

bokal   *bokal*

javelin

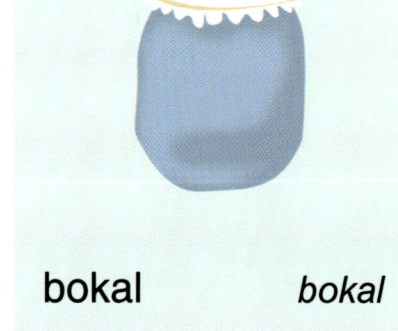

frenn   *frinhn*

jaw

machwè   *machweh*

jeans

djins   *djeens*

jelly

jele   *jele*

jetty

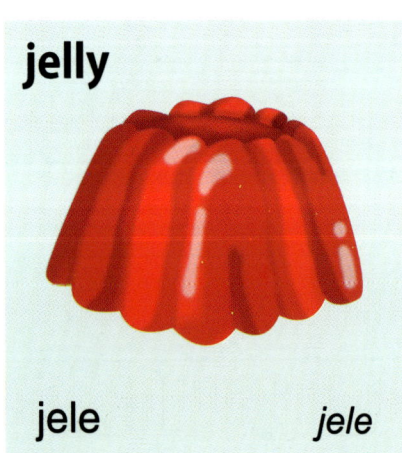

waf   *waf*

jewellery
US English **jewelry**

bijou   *beejoo*

jigsaw

pilz *peelz*

jockey

joke *joke*

joker

jokè *jokeh*

journey

vwayaj *vwayaj*

jug

krich *kreech*

juggler

jonglè *jonhgleh*

juice

ji *jee*

jungle

jeng *jinhg*

jute

jit *jeet*

Kk

kangaroo

kangouwou *kanhgoowoo*

kennel

nich *neech*

kerb
US English **curb**

arebò twotwa
areboh twotwa

kerosene

kewozèn
kewozehn

ketchup

sòs tomat
sohs tomat

kettle

chodyè　　*chodyeh*

key

kle　　*kle*

keyboard

klavye　　*klavye*

key ring

twouse kle
twooso kle

kidney

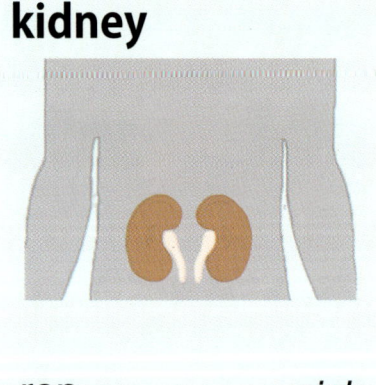

ren　　*rinh*

kilogram

kilogram
keelogram

king

wa　　*wa*

kiosk

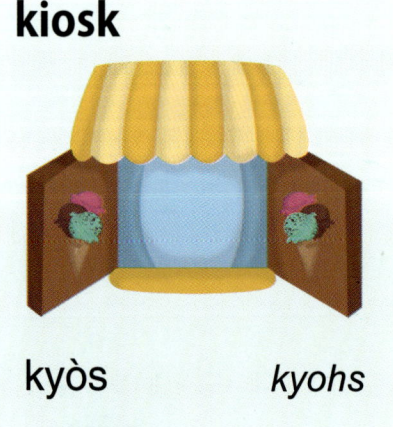

kyòs　　*kyohs*

kiss

ti bo　　*tee bo*

kitchen

kizin *keezeen*

kite

kap *kap*

kitten

chat *chat*

kiwi

kiwi *keewee*

knee

jenou *jenoo*

knife

kouto *kooto*

knight

chevalye *chevalye*

knitwear

triko *treeko*

knob

bouton seri *bootonh seree*

knock

frape *frape*

knot

ne *ne*

knuckle

atikilasyon *ateekeelasyonh*

a b c d e f g h i j **k** l m n o p q r s t u v w x y z

Ll

label

etikèt *eteekeht*

laboratory

laboratwa *laboratwa*

lace

lasèt *laseht*

ladder

nechèl *nechehl*

lady

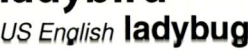

madam *madam*

ladybird
US English **ladybug**

koksinèl *kokseenehl*

lagoon

lagon *lagonh*

lake

lak *lak*

lamb

ti mouton *tee mootonh*

lamp

lanp *lanhp*

lamp post

poto limyè *poto leemyeh*

a b c d e f g h i j k **l** m n o p q r s t u v w x y z

land

teren   *terinh*

lane

tras   *tras*

lantern

lantèn   *lanhtehn*

laser

lazè   *lazeh*

lasso

lans   *lanhs*

latch

takèt   *takeht*

laundry

lesiv   *leseev*

lawn

gazon   *gazonh*

lawyer

avoka   *avoka*

layer

kouch   *kooch*

leaf

fèy   *fehy*

leather

kwi   *kwee*

51

a b c d e f g h i J k **l** m n o p q r s t u v w x y z

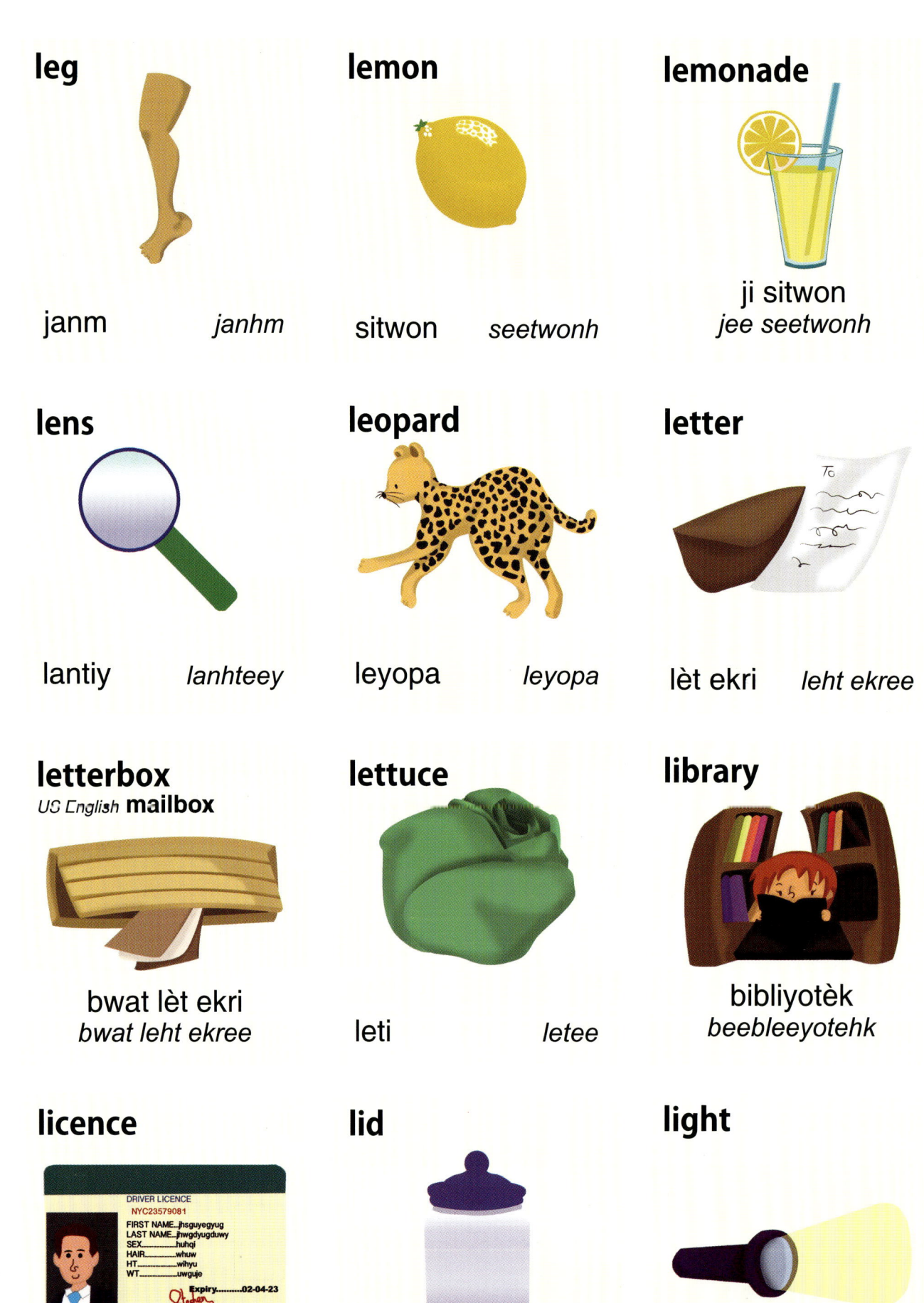

leg

janm *janhm*

lemon

sitwon *seetwonh*

lemonade

ji sitwon
jee seetwonh

lens

lantiy *lanhteey*

leopard

leyopa *leyopa*

letter

lèt ekri *leht ekree*

letterbox
US English **mailbox**

bwat lèt ekri
bwat leht ekree

lettuce

leti *letee*

library

bibliyotèk
beebleeyotehk

licence

lisans *leesans*

lid

kouvèti *koovehtee*

light

limyè *leemyeh*

lighthouse
fa *fa*

limb
manm *manhm*

line
liy *leey*

lion
lyon *lyonh*

lip
lèv *lehv*

lipstick
woujalèv *woojalehv*

liquid
likid *leekeed*

list
lis *lees*

litre
US English **liter**
lit *leet*

living room
salon *salonh*

lizard
zandolit *zanhdoleet*

load
pakèt *pakeht*

a b c d e f g h i J k **l** m n o p q r s t u v w x y z

a
b
c
d
e
f
g
h
i
J
k
l
m
n
o
p
q
r
s
t
u
v
w
x
y
z

loaf

pen   *pinh*

lobster

oma   *oma*

lock

kadna   *kadna*

loft

galata   *galata*

log

bout bwa
bootbwa

loop

bouk   *book*

lorry

US English **truck**

kamyon   *kamyonh*

lotus

lotis   *lotees*

louse

pou   *poo*

luggage

chay   *chay*

lunch

manje midi
manhje meedee

lung

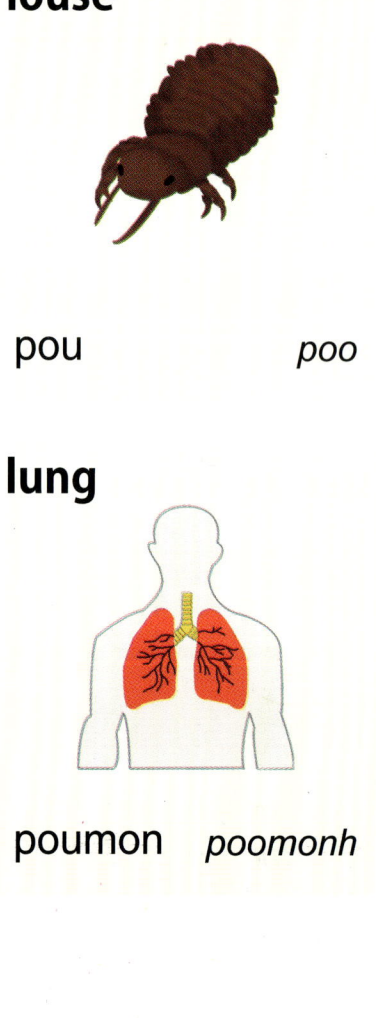

poumon   *poomonh*

Mm

machine

machin *macheen*

magazine

magazin *magazeen*

magician

majisyen *majeesyinh*

magnet

leman *lemanh*

magpie

yon zwazo *yon zwaso*

mail
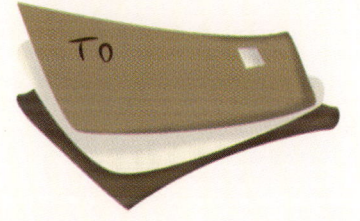
lapòs *lapohs*

mammal

mamifè *mameefeh*

man

nonm *nonhm*

mandolin

mandolin *manhdoleen*

mango

mango *mango*

map

kat jewografi *kat jewografee*

a b c d e f g h i j k l m n o p q r s t u v w x y z

a b c d e f g h i j J k l m n o p q r s t u v w x y z

maple

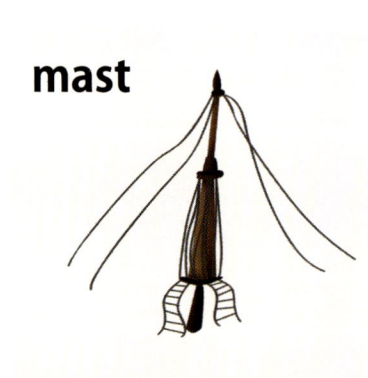

erab   *erab*

marble

mab   *mab*

market

mache   *mache*

mask

mas   *mas*

mast

ma bato   *mabato*

mat

kapèt   *kapeht*

matchbox

bwat alimèt
bwat aleemeht

mattress

matla   *matla*

meal

repa   *repa*

meat

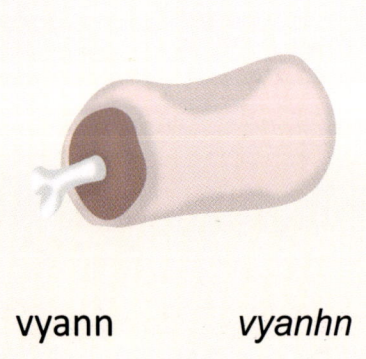

vyann   *vyanhn*

mechanic

mekanisyen
mekaneesyenh

medicine

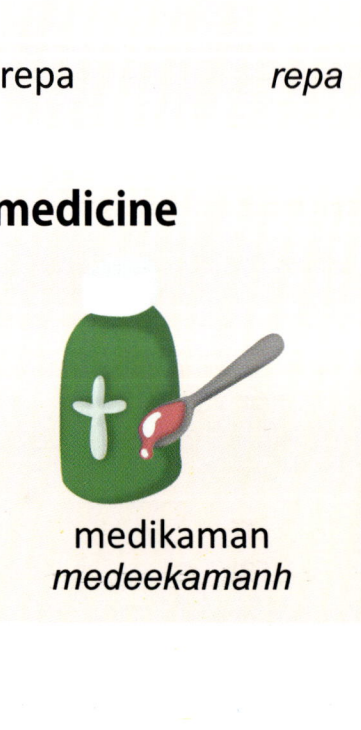

medikaman
medeekamanh

melon

melon   *melonh*

merchant

machann
machanhn

mermaid

sirèn   *seerehn*

metal

metal   *metal*

metre

US English **meter**

mèt   *meht*

microphone

mikwo   *meekwo*

microwave

mikwo ond
meekwo onhd

mile

mil   *meel*

milk

lèt   *leht*

miner

travayè min
travayè meen

mineral

mineral   *meeneral*

mint

mant   *manht*

minute

minit   *meeneet*

mirror

glas   *glas*

mobile phone

telefòn mobil
telefohn mobeel

model

modèl   *modehl*

mole

mol   *mol*

money

lajan   *lajanh*

monk

mwàn   *mwan*

monkey

makak   *makak*

monster

mons   *monhs*

month

mwa   *mwa*

monument

moniman
moneemanh

moon

lalin   *laleen*

mop

mòp *mohp*

morning

maten *matenh*

mosquito

marengwen
marinhgwinh

moth

gwo papiyon
gwo papeeyonh

mother

manman
manhmanh

motorcycle

motosiklèt
motoseekleht

motorway

otowout *otowoot*

mountain

mòn *mòn*

mouse

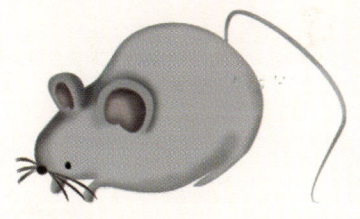

sourit *sooreet*

mousetrap

ratyè *ratyeh*

moustache

moustach
moostach

mouth

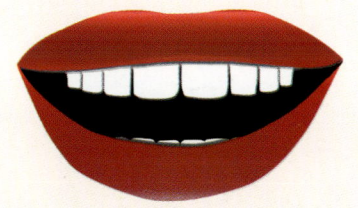

bouch *booch*

a b c d e f g h i J k l m n o p q r s t u v w x y z

mud

labou *laboo*

muffin

mòfin *mohfeen*

mug

gwo tas *gwo tas*

mule

milèt *meeleht*

muscle

misk *meesk*

museum

mize *meeze*

mushroom

djondjon
djonhdjonh

music

mizik *meezeek*

musician

mizisyen
meezeesyenh

Nn

nail

klou *kloo*

napkin

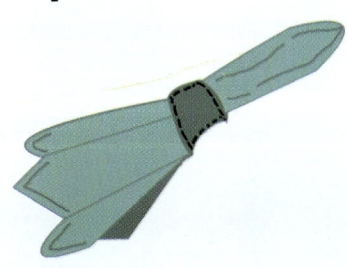

napkin *napkeen*

nappy
US English **diaper**

daypè *daypeh*

nature

lanati *lanatee*

neck

kou *koo*

necklace

kolye *kolye*

necktie

kòl *kohl*

needle

zegwi *zegwee*

neighbour
US English **neighbor**

vwazen *vwazinh*

nest

nich *neech*

net

filè *feeleh*

newspaper

jounal *joonal*

night

lannwit *lannweet*

nine

nèf *nehf*

a b c d e f g h i J k l m **n** o p q r s t u v w x y z

noodles

nouy   *nooy*

noon

midi   *meedee*

north

nò   *noh*

nose

nen   *ninh*

note

nòt   *noht*

notebook

kaye   *kaye*

notice

avi   *avee*

number

nimewo   *neemewo*

nun

mè   *meh*

nurse

enfimyè   *inhfeemyeh*

nursery

krèch   *krehch*

nut

nwa   *nwa*

a b c d e f g h i J k l m **n** o p q r s t u v w x y z

Oo

oar

ram *ram*

observatory

obsèvatwa *obsehvatwa*

ocean

lanmè *lanhmeh*

octopus

chat wouj *chat wooj*

office

biwo *beewo*

oil

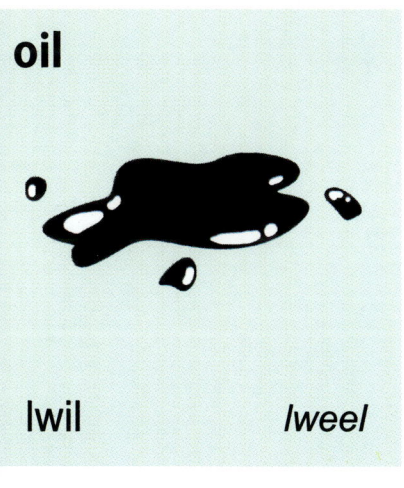

lwil *lweel*

olive

oliv *oleev*

omelette

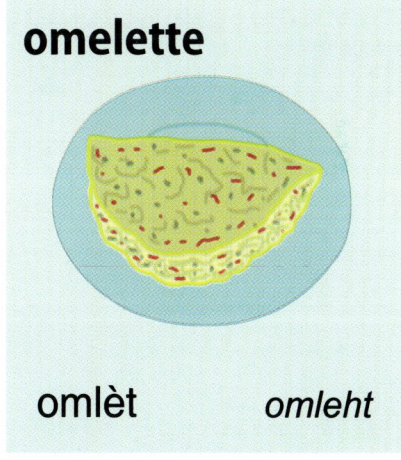

omlèt *omleht*

one

youn *yoon*

onion

zonyon *zonhyonh*

orange

zoranj *zoranhj*

a b c d e f g h i J k l m n o p q r s t u v w x y z

orbit

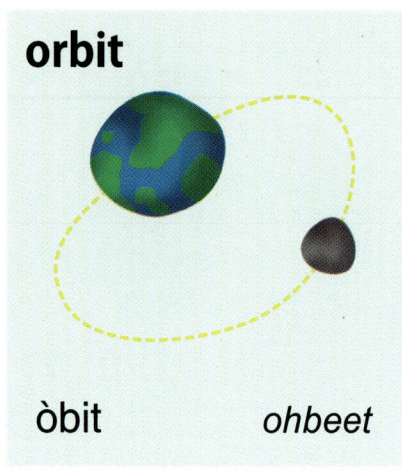

òbit   *ohbeet*

orchard

plantasyon fwi
planhtasyonh fwee

orchestra

òkès   *ohkehs*

ostrich

otrich   *otreech*

otter

lout   *loot*

oval

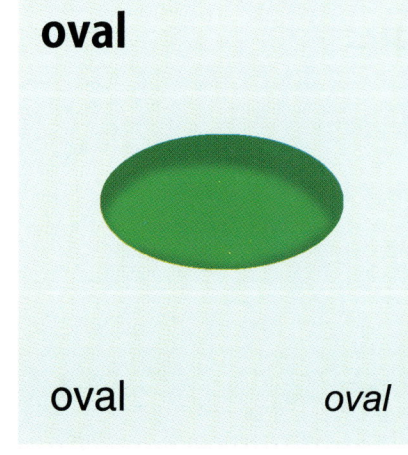

oval   *oval*

oven

fou   *foo*

owl

koukou   *kookoo*

ox

towo bèf
towo behf

Pp

packet

pakèt   *pakeht*

page

paj   *paj*

pain

doulè   *dooleh*

paint

penti   *pinhtee*

painting

tablo   *tablo*

pair

pè   *peh*

palace

palè   *paleh*

palm

pla men   *pla minh*

pan

kaswòl   *kaswohl*

pancake

galèt   *galeht*

panda

panda   *panhda*

papaya

papay   *papay*

paper

papye   *papye*

parachute

parachit   *paracheet*

a b c d e f g h i j k l m n o **p** q r s t u v w x y z

parcel

pakè *pakeh*

park

pak *pak*

parrot

jako *jako*

passenger

pasaje *pasaje*

pasta

pat *pat*

pastry

patisri *pateesree*

pavement

twotwa *twotwa*

paw

pat *pat*

pea

pwa *pwa*

peach

pèch *pehch*

peacock

pan *panh*

peak

pwent *pwinht*

peanut

pistach *peestach*

pear

pwa *pwa*

pearl

grenn pèl
grinhn pehl

pedal

pedal *pedal*

pelican

pelikan *peleekanh*

pen

plim *pleem*

pencil

kreyon *kreyonh*

penguin

pengwen
pingwinh

pepper

pwav *pwav*

perfume

pafen *pafinh*

pet

bèt kay *beht kay*

pharmacy

famasi *famasee*

a b c d e f g h i j k l m n o p q r s t u v w x y z

a b c d e f g h i J k l m n o p q r s t u v w x y z

photograph

foto *foto*

piano

pyano *pyano*

picture

imaj *eemaj*

pie

tat *tat*

pig

kochon *kochonh*

pigeon

pijon *peejonh*

pillar

pilye *peelye*

pillow

zòrye *zohrye*

pilot

pilòt *peeloht*

pineapple

anana *anana*

pink

woz *woz*

pipe

tiyo *teeyo*

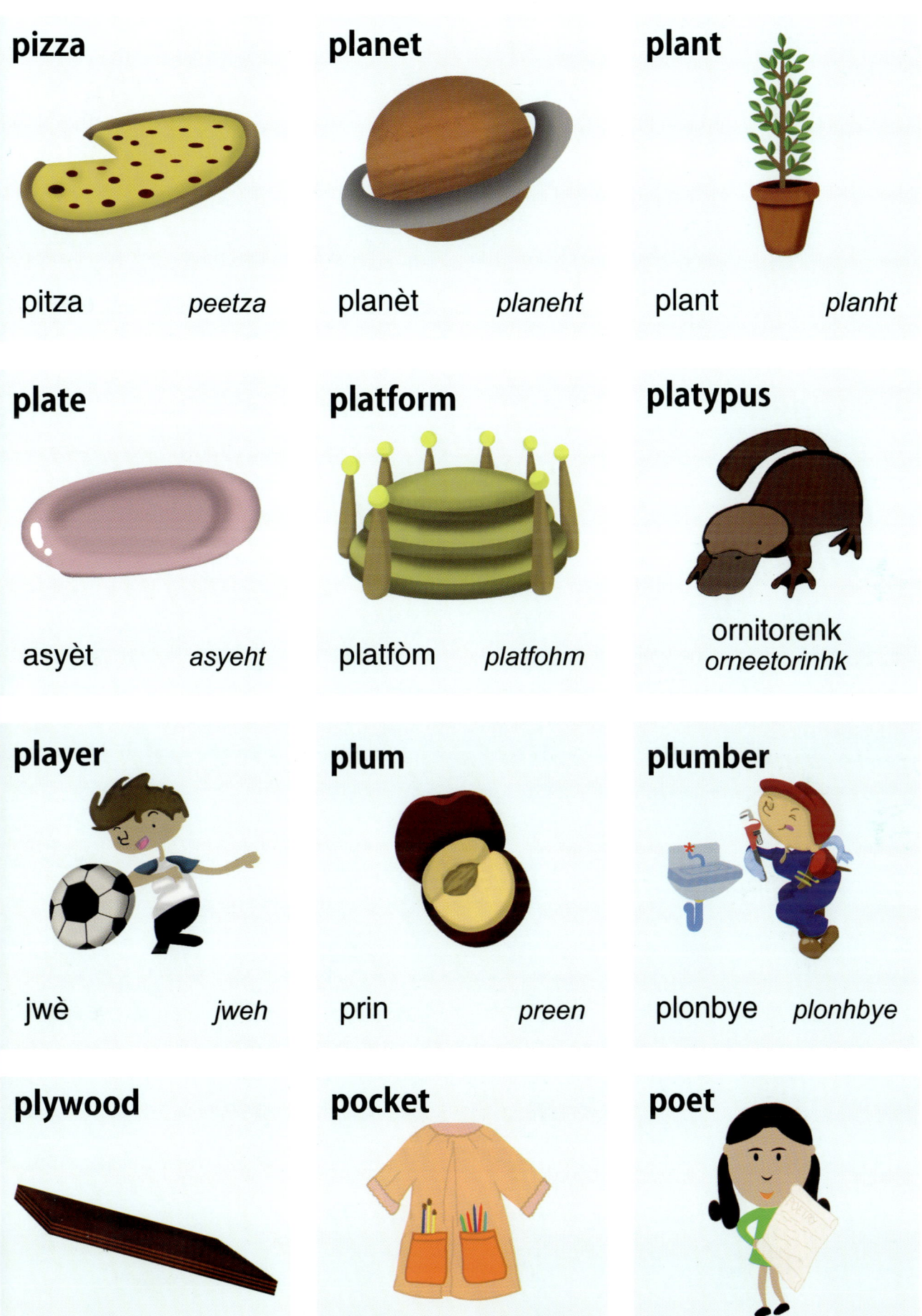

pizza

pitza *peetza*

planet

planèt *planeht*

plant

plant *planht*

plate

asyèt *asyeht*

platform

platfòm *platfohm*

platypus

ornitorenk *orneetorinhk*

player

jwè *jweh*

plum

prin *preen*

plumber

plonbye *plonhbye*

plywood

playwoud *playwood*

pocket

pòch *pohch*

poet

powèt *poweht*

a
b
c
d
e
f
g
h
i
J
k
l
m
n
o
p
q
r
s
t
u
v
w
x
y
z

a b c d e f g h i j J k l m n o **p** q r s t u v w x y z

polar bear

lous polè
loos poleh

police

lapolis   *lapolees*

pollution

polisyon
poleesyon

pomegranate

grenad   *grenad*

pond

ma dlo   *madlo*

porcupine

pòkipin
pohkeepeen

port

pò   *poh*

porter

potè   *poteh*

postcard

kat postal
kat postal

postman

faktè   *fakteh*

post office

lapòs   *lapohs*

pot

po   *po*

potato

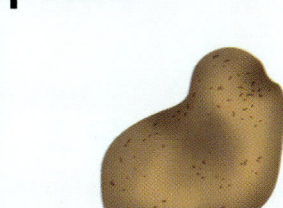

pòmtè   *pohmteh*

powder

poud   *pood*

prawn
US English **shrimp**

krevèt   *kreveht*

priest

prèt   *preht*

prince

prens   *prinhs*

prison

prizon   *preezonh*

pudding

pòding   *pohding*

pump

ponp   *ponhp*

pumpkin

joumou   *joomoo*

puppet

maryonèt
maryoneht

puppy

ti chen   *tee chinh*

purse

bous   *boos*

a b c d e f g h i J k l m n o **p** q r s t u v w x y z

Qq

quail

kay *kay*

quarry

karyè sab
karyeh sab

queen

larenn *larinhn*

queue

nan liy *nanh leey*

quiver

kakwa *kakwa*

Rr

rabbit

lapen *lapinh*

rack

etajè *etajeh*

racket

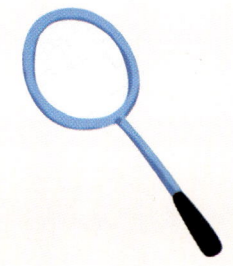

rakèt *rakeht*

radio

radyo *radyo*

radish

radi *radee*

raft

rado *rado*

rain

lapli *laplee*

rainbow

lakansyèl
lakanhsyehl

raisin

rezen *rezinh*

ramp

ranp *ranhp*

raspberry

franbwaz
franhbwaz

rat

rat *rat*

razor

razwa *razwa*

receipt

resi *resee*

rectangle

rektang *rektanhg*

red

wouj *wooj*

restaurant

restoran
restoranh

a b c d e f g h i J k l m n o p q r s t u v w x y z

a b c d e f g h i j J k l m n o p q r s t u v w x y z

rhinoceros

rinoseròs
reenoserohs

rib

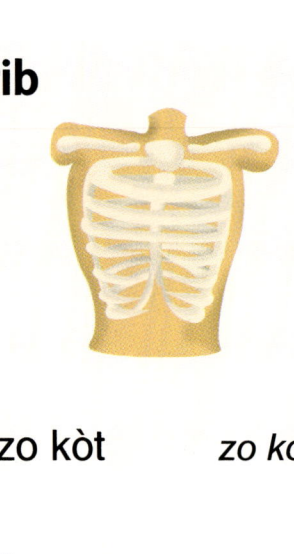

zo kòt   *zo koht*

ribbon

zo kòt   *zo koht*

riban   *reebanh*

rice

diri   *deeree*

ring

bag   *bag*

river

rivyè   *reevyeh*

road

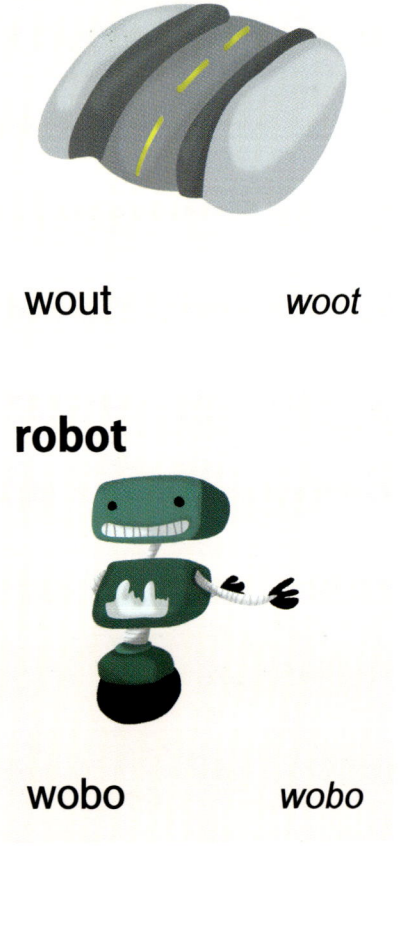

wout   *woot*

robber

vòlè   *vohleh*

robe

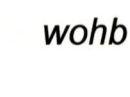

wòb   *wohb*

robot

wobo   *wobo*

rock

wòch   *wohch*

rocket

fize   *feeze*

roller coaster

wolè kostè
woleh kosteh

room

chanm   *chanhm*

root

rasin   *raseen*

rope

kòd   *kohd*

rose

woz   *woz*

round

wonn   *wonhn*

rug

tapi   *tapee*

rugby

rigbi   *reegbee*

ruler

règ   *règ*

Ss

sack

sak   *sak*

sail

navige   *naveege*

a b c d e f g h i j k l m n o p q r s t u v w x y z

sailor

maren *marinh*

salad

salad *salad*

salt

sèl *sehl*

sand

sab *sab*

sandwich

sandwitch
sanhdweetch

satellite

satelit *sateleet*

saucer

soukoup *sookoop*

sausage

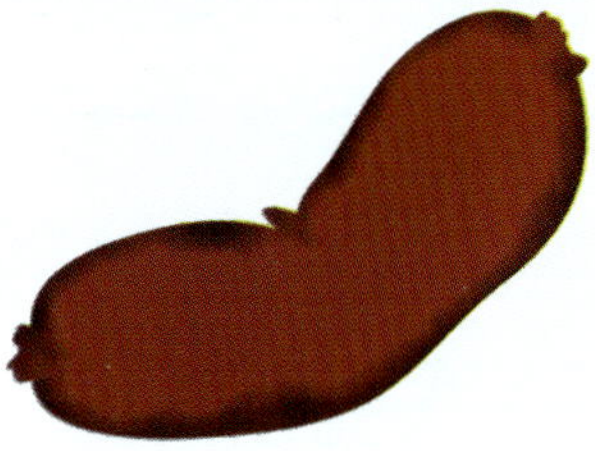

sosis *sosees*

saw

si *see*

scarf

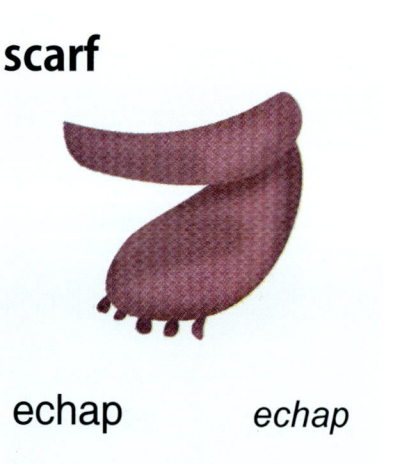

echap *echap*

school

lekòl *lekohl*

scissors

sizo *seezo*

scooter

twotinèt
twoteeneh

scorpion

eskòpyon
eskohpyonh

screw

vis   *vees*

sea

lanmè   *lanhmeh*

seal

fòk   *fohk*

seat

syèj   *syehj*

see-saw

balanswa
balanhswa

seven

sèt   *seht*

shadow

lonbraj   *lonhbraj*

shampoo

chanpou
chanhpou

shark

reken   *rekinh*

sheep

mouton   *mootonh*

a b c d e f g h i J k l m n o p q r **s** t u v w x y z

a b c d e f g h i J K l m n o p q r **s** t u v w x y z

shelf

etajè   *etajeh*

shell

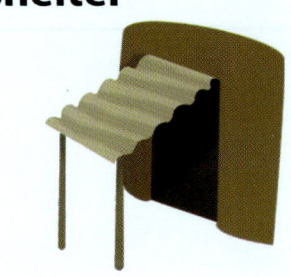

kokiy   *kokeey*

shelter

abri   *abree*

ship

bato   *bato*

shirt

chemiz   *chemeez*

shoe

soulye   *soolye*

shorts

bout chòt
boot choht

shoulder

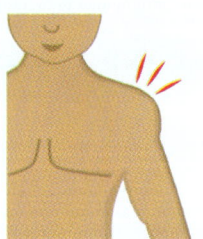

zepòl   *zepohl*

shower

douch   *dooch*

shutter

panofenèt
panofeneht

shuttlecock

boul batminton
bool batmeenton

signal

siyal   *seeyal*

silver

ajan *ajanh*

sink

lavabo *lavabo*

sister

sè *seh*

six

sis *sees*

skate

paten *patinh*

skeleton

eskelèt *eskeleht*

ski

eski *eskee*

skin

po *po*

skirt

jip *jeep*

skull

zo kràn *zo kran*

sky

syèl *syehl*

skyscraper

gratsyèl *gratsyehl*

a b c d e f g h i J k l m n o p q r **s** t u v w x y z

slide

glisad   *gleesad*

slipper

pantouf   *panhtoof*

smoke

lafimen   *lafeeminh*

snail

kalmason
kalmasonh

snake

koulèv   *koolehv*

snow

nèj   *nehj*

soap

savon   *savonh*

sock

chosèt   *choseht*

sofa

sofa   *sofa*

soil

tè   *teh*

soldier

sòlda   *sohlda*

soup

soup   *soop*

space

espas   *espas*

spaghetti

espageti
espagetee

sphere

esfè   *esfeh*

spider

arenye   *arenye*

spinach

zepina   *zepeena*

sponge

eponj   *eponhj*

spoon

kiyè   *keeyeh*

spray

esprey   *esprey*

spring

prentan   *prinhtanh*

square

kare   *kare*

squirrel

ekirèy   *ekeerehy*

stadium

estad   *estad*

a b c d e f g h i J k l m n o p q r **s** t u v w x y z

a b c d e f g h i J k l m n o p q r s t u v w x y z

stairs

eskalye   *eskalye*

stamp

tenb   *tinhb*

star

zetwal   *zetwal*

station

estasyon
estasyonh

statue

estati   *estatee*

stethoscope

estetoskòp
estetoskohp

stomach

estomak   *estomak*

stone

wòch   *wohch*

storm

tanpèt   *tanhpeht*

straw

chalimo   *chaleemo*

strawberry

frèz   *frehz*

street

lari   *laree*

student

etidyan
eteedyanh

submarine

soumaren
soomarinh

subway

tren   *trinh*

sugar

sik   *seek*

sugarcane

kann   *kanhn*

summer

lete   *lete*

sun

solèy   *solehy*

supermarket

makèt   *makeht*

swan

siy   *seey*

sweet

dous   *doos*

swimming pool

pisin   *peeseen*

swimsuit

mayo benyen
mayo binhyinh

a b c d e f g h i j k l m n o p q r s t u v w x y z

swing

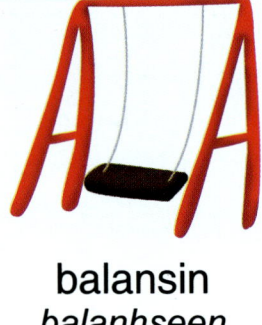

balansin
balanhseen

switch

bouton limyè
bootonh leemyeh

syrup

siwo　　*seewo*

Tt

table

tab　　*tab*

tall

wo　　*wo*

tank

chadegè
chadegeh

taxi

taksi　　*taksee*

tea

te　　*te*

teacher

pwofesè　*pwofeseh*

teeth

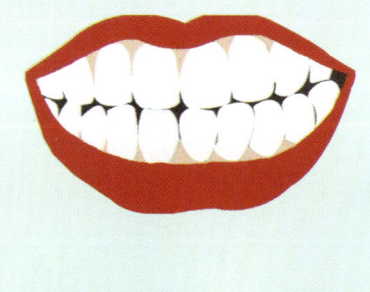

dan　　*danh*

telephone

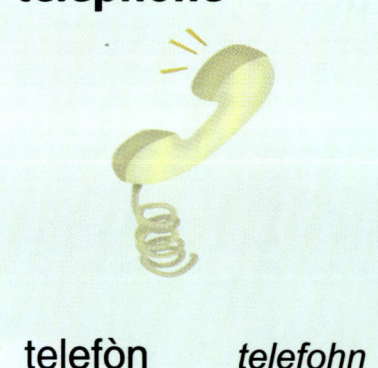

telefòn　*telefohn*

television

televizyon
televeezyonh

ten

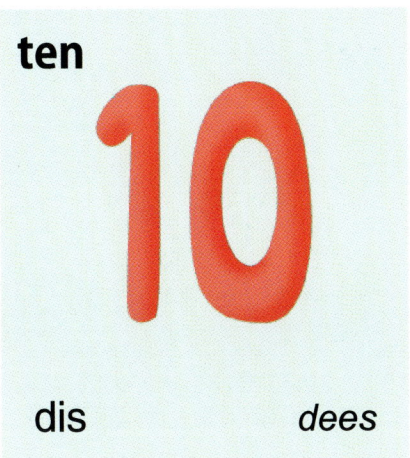

dis   *dees*

tennis

tenis   *tenees*

tent

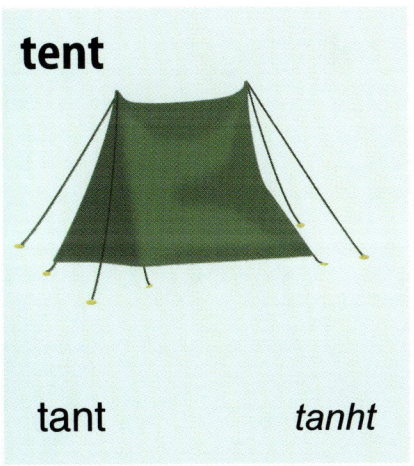

tant   *tanht*

thief

vòlè   *vohleh*

thread

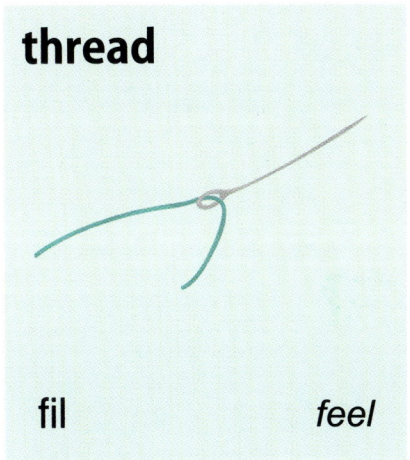

fil   *feel*

three

twa   *twa*

throat

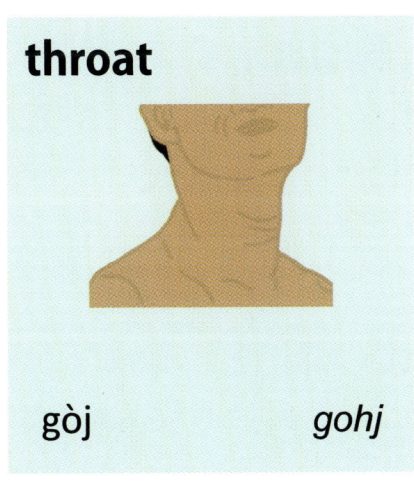

gòj   *gohj*

thumb

gwo pous
gwo poos

ticket

biyè   *beeyeh*

tiger

tig   *teeg*

toe

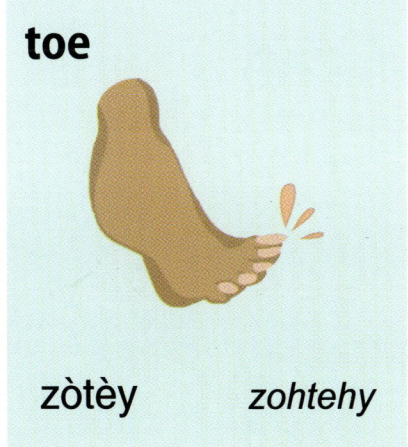

zòtèy   *zohtehy*

a b c d e f g h i j k l m n o p q r s **t** u v w x y z

tofu

tofou *tofoo*

tomato

tomat *tomat*

tongue

lang *lanhg*

tool

zouti *zootee*

toothbrush

bwòs dan
bwohs danh

toothpaste

pat *pat*

tortoise

tòti *tohtee*

towel

sèvyèt *sehvyeht*

tower

tou *too*

toy

jwèt *jweht*

tractor

traktè *trakteh*

train

tren *trinh*

a b c d e f g h i j J k l m n o p q r s **t** u v w x y z

tree

pyebwa *pyebwa*

triangle

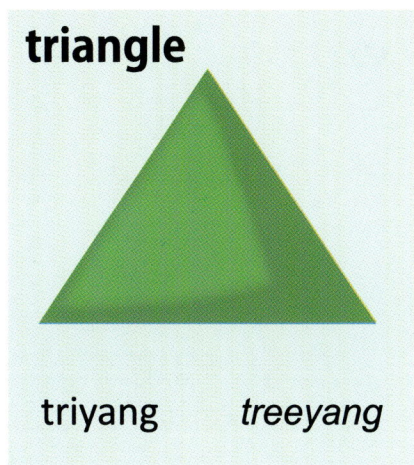

triyang *treeyang*

tub

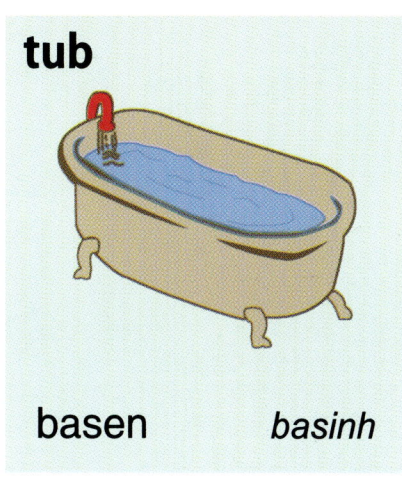

basen *basinh*

tunnel

tinèl *teenehl*

turnip

navèt *naveht*

tyre

US English **tire**

kawotchou
kawotchoo

umbrella

parapli *paraplee*

uncle

tonton *tonhtonh*

uniform

inifòm *eeneefohm*

university

inivèsite
eeneevehseete

utensil

veso *veso*

a b c d e f g h i J k l m n o p q r s **t** u v w x y z

Vv

vacuum cleaner

aspiratè
aspeerateh

valley

vale *vale*

van

kamyonèt
kamyoneht

vase

vaz *vaz*

vault

vout *voot*

vegetable

legim *legeem*

veil

vwal *vwal*

vet

veterinè *veterineh*

village

bouk *book*

violet

vyolèt *vyoleht*

violin

vyolon *vyolonh*

a b c d e f g h i J k l m n o p q r s t u v w x y z

volcano

vòlkan *vohlkanh*

volleyball

volebòl *volebohl*

vulture

votou *votoo*

Ww

waist

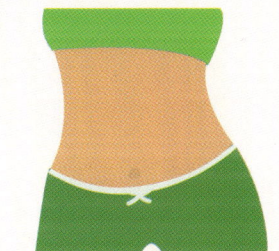

senti *sinhtee*

waitress

sèvez *sehvez*

wall

mi *mee*

wallet

bous *boos*

walnut

nwa *nwa*

wand

bagèt *bagueht*

wardrobe

amwa *amwa*

warehouse

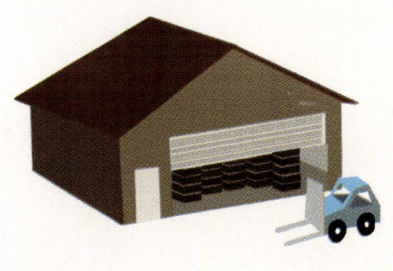

depo *depo*

a b c d e f g h i J k l m n o p q r s t u **v** **w** x y z

wasp

gèp *guehp*

watch

gade *gade*

water

dlo *dlo*

watermelon

melon *melonh*

web

twal arenye
twal arenye

whale

balèn *balehn*

wheat

ble *ble*

wheel

wou *woo*

whistle

souflèt *soofleht*

white

blan *blanh*

wife

madanm *madanhm*

window

fenèt *feneht*

a b c d e f g h i j k l m n o p q r s t u v **w** x y z

wing

zèl *zehl*

winter

livè *leeveh*

wizard

majisyen
majeesyinh

wolf

lou *loo*

woman

fanm *fanhm*

woodpecker

sèpantye
sèpanhtye

wool

lenn *linhn*

workshop

atelye *atelye*

wrist

pwanyè *pwanyeh*

Xx

x-ray

radyografi
radyografee

xylophone

zilofòn *zeelofohn*

a b c d e f g h i J k l m n o p q r s t u v w x y z

a b c d e f g h i J k l m n o p q r s t u v w x **y** **z**

Yy

yacht

yatch   *yatch*

yak

yak   *yak*

yard

lakou   *lakoo*

yellow

jòn   *john*

yoghurt

yawout   *yawoot*

Zz

zebra
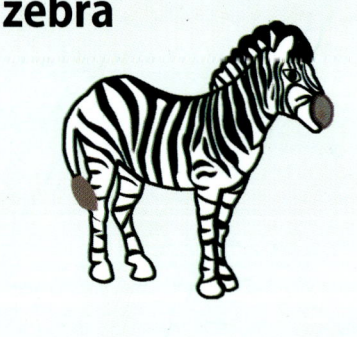
zèb   *zehb*

zero

zewo   *zewo*

zip

zip   *zeep*

zodiac

zodyak   *zodyak*

zoo

zou   *zoo*